The Associate

by Simon Bent

TRANSFORMATION

29 April–21 September 2002

The Lyttelton *Transformation* project is vital to my idea of the
National Theatre because it both celebrates and challenges our
identity. What do we want the National to be? We must draw on
our heritage, on our recent past, and on the talent of the next
generation. I want a thriving new audience, including a body
of young people under 30 with a theatre-going habit, a new
generation of artistic and administrative talent committed to
taking the National forward and a realization of the varied
potential within this glorious building.

Trevor Nunn Director of the National Theatre

Transformation is thirteen world premieres, hosted in two new
theatre spaces, with special low ticket prices. The National's most
traditional auditorium, the Lyttelton, has been transformed by
a sweep of seats from circle to stage to create a new intimacy
between actor and audience. At the same time the Loft has been
created – a fully flexible 100-seat theatre. *Transformation* will
introduce new generations of theatre makers and theatre
audiences to one of the most exciting theatres in the world.

Mick Gordon Artistic Associate
Joseph Smith Associate Producer

Transformation has received major creative input from the Studio –
the National Theatre's laboratory for new work and its engine
room for new writing – and celebrates the Studio's continuing
investment in theatre makers.

The Associate

by Simon Bent

In order of speaking

Ray	NICOLAS TENNANT
Watson	JOHN NORMINGTON
Tiny	MATTHEW RHYS

Director	PAUL MILLER
Designer	JACKIE BROOKS
Lighting Designer	CATRIONA SILVER
Sound Designer	RICH WALSH
Company Voice Work	PATSY RODENBURG & KATE GODFREY

Assistant Director	Timothy Stark
Production Manager	Katrina Gilroy
Stage Manager	Fiona Greenhill
Deputy Stage Manager	Sally McKenna
Assistant Stage Manager	Alison Biggs
Assistant Designer	Holly Blenkins
Costume Supervisor	Frances Gager, assisted by Louise Bratton
Casting	Hannah Miller

OPENING: Loft 19 August 2002

NATIONAL THEATRE BOOKSHOP
The National's Bookshop in the Main Entrance foyer on the ground floor stocks a wide range of theatre-related books. Texts of all the plays in the Loft during the Transformation season, and of the plays in Channels (France) are available from the NT Bookshop at £2, and Simon Bent's stage version of A Prayer for Owen Meany, which is also available at £2 exclusively from the National's Bookshop, and only until the end of Transformation. T: 020 7452 3456; www.nationaltheatre.org.uk/bookshop

Copies of this cast list in braille or large print are available at the Information Desk

JOHN NORMINGTON
WATSON

Training: Northern School of Music. **Theatre** work for the NT, RSC and West End includes *The Homecoming, Wars of the Roses, Guys and Dolls, Danton's Death, The Fool, As You Like It, The Master Builder, The Mysteries, The Winter's Tale, The Good Hope* and most recently *Original Sin* at the Sheffield Crucible, directed by Peter Gill. **Television:** *Inspector Morse, The Bill, Hercules Poirot, Dr Who, Casualty, Preston Front.* **Radio:** *Jude the Obscure* and *Amadeus.* **Film:** *A Private Function, Stardust, Rollerball* and *The Medusa Touch.*

MATTHEW RHYS
TINY

Matthew Rhys was born and raised in South Wales and educated in his native tongue – Welsh. He won a scholarship to RADA. His first professional **theatre** debut was at the National Theatre in Peter Gill's *Cardiff East.* Most recently he appeared opposite Kathleen Turner in *The Graduate.* Matthew Rhys has appeared in several television dramas and feature films including *Tabloid* with John Hurt, to be released in autumn 2002.

NICOLAS TENNANT
RAY

Recent **theatre** credits include Tosser in *A Carpet, A Pony & A Monkey* (The Bush); *A Christmas Carol* and *The Recruiting Officer* (Chichester); *Comedians* (Oxford Stage); *Action* (Young Vic); *Herons* (Royal Court); *Les Justes* (Gate); *King Lear* (RSC); *Little Malcolm and His Struggle Against the Eunuchs* (HTC & West End); *Sugar Sugar, Love and Understanding* and *Bad Company* (The Bush). Film includes *Tube Tales, Oscar and Lucinda, Backbeat, The Gift, The Fool* and *A Dangerous Man.* **Television** includes *Residents, Back-Up, The Bill, The Bombmaker, Between The Lines, Friday On My Mind, Trainer* and *Nice Town.*

SIMON BENT
WRITER
Simon Bent's plays include an adaptation of John Irving's *A Prayer for Owen Meany* (NT Transformation season), Full Fathom Five, The Trouble with Girls, (NT Studio), Wasted (Old Red Lion), Bad Company, Goldhawk Road, Sugar Sugar (The Bush), Shelter (BT Connections/NT), Accomplices (Sheffield Crucible) and a screenplay for the **film** Christie Malry's Own Double Entry.

PAUL MILLER
DIRECTOR
Paul Miller has worked extensively at the National's **Studio** and is Resident Director of the Loft Theatre. Recent productions include Mean Tears by Peter Gill (Sheffield Crucible); Four Nights in Knaresborough by Paul Webb (national tour); Tragedy: A Tragedy by Will Eno (Gate); Accomplices by Simon Bent and Mr England by Richard Bean (Sheffield Crucible); Unsinkable by Richard Bean (Radio 3); A Penny for a Song by John Whiting (Oxford Stage Co/Whitehall); Hushabye Mountain by Jonathan Harvey (ETT/Hampstead) and Simon Bent's plays Sugar Sugar, Goldhawk Road and Bad Company (Bush).

JACKIE BROOKS
DESIGNER
Jackie Brooks's theatre work includes Accomplices and Mr England (Sheffield Crucible); Hushabye Mountain (Hampstead Theatre and tour); Shellfish, A Difficult Age, The School for Scandal, Rupert Street Lonely Hearts Club, The School for Wives and The Beaux' Stratagem (English Touring Theatre); Present Laughter (Aarhus Theatre, Denmark); Rosmersholm, Seascape with Sharks and Dancer (Southwark Playhouse); Strindberg's Chamber Plays (Gate Theatre) and The Neighbour, Street Trash, and Hurricane Roses (NT Studio and Cottesloe). Film and television work includes Wet and Dry, Favourite and The Linesman.

Opera includes Albert Herring, Die Entführung aus dem Serail and Don Giovanni (Garsington).

CATRIONA SILVER
LIGHTING DESIGNER
Catriona Silver specialises in theatrical and architectural lighting and will soon graduate with an MSc in Light and Lighting. Architectural lighting designs include Container City at Trinity Buoy Wharf and Interior lighting for Hermés. **Theatre** lighting designs include Sweeney Todd at the Bristol Old Vic, The Crucible for The Oxford School of Drama, Picasso's Women in The Cottesloe, Twelve Angry Men at the Garage Theatre, and Peter Pan, Just Between Ourselves, Dead Funny, Lend me a Tenor and The Hollow at the Palace Theatre, Southend.

RICH WALSH
SOUND DESIGNER
Previous sound designs include: The Mentalists, The Shadow of a Boy, Free, Sing Yer Heart Out for the Lads, The Walls (National), Exposure, Under The Blue Sky, On Raftery's Hill, Sacred Heart, Trust, Choice (Royal Court); Julie Burchill is Away (Soho Theatre); 50 Revolutions (Whitehall); The Boy Who Left Home, The Nation's Favourite (UK tours), Yllana's 666 (Riverside Studios); Strike Gently Away From Body, Blavatsky (Young Vic Studio); Body And Soul, Soap Opera, The Baltimore Waltz (Upstairs At The Gatehouse), Small Craft Warnings (Pleasance); The Taming of the Shrew, Macbeth (Japanese tour); Dirk, Red Noses (Oxford Playhouse); The Wizard of Oz, The Winter's Tale (Old Fire Station, Oxford).

TIMOTHY STARK
ASSISTANT DIRECTOR
Recipient of this year's Cohen Bursary at the NT Studio. Most recently, for the NT Transformation season, co-directed with Mick Gordon Le Pub! (Channels), and assisted on A Prayer for Owen Meany (NT Transformation season), and Push Up (Royal Court). **Directing** includes Bombing People and Signing Off (Jermyn St Theatre); Dealt With (Chelsea Centre); Heads (Bridewell); Serving It Up, Rafts and Dreams, King John (Poor School). Also directed a workshop of Metro, a new musical which he co-wrote. **Acting** credits include The Natural Cause (NT Studio); Across Oka, Mary and Lizzy and Restoration (RSC); Making Noise Quietly and Macbeth (RSC/Almeida); A Memory of Two Mondays (Cockpit); Les Liaisons Dangereuses (Derby); Neville South's Washbag (Finborough). **TV**: Guardians, Pie in the Sky, Frankenstein, All Good Things, William Tell, Little Eyolf. **Film**: Heaven's Promise and A Shocking Accident.

The Loft Theatre was created with the help of the Royal National Theatre Foundation.

Many of the projects in the *Transformation* season were developed in the National Theatre Studio.

The Transformation season is supported by Edward and Elissa Annunziato, Peter Wolff Theatre Trust, and by a gift from the estate of André Deutsch.

ON WORD graphics designed by typographer Alan Kitching using original wood letters.

TRANSFORMATION SEASON TEAM
ARTISTIC ASSOCIATE Mick Gordon
ASSOCIATE PRODUCER Joseph Smith
ADMINISTRATOR Sarah Nicholson
LOFT THEATRE DESIGNER Will Bowen
FRONT OF HOUSE DESIGNER Jo Maund
FRONT OF HOUSE DESIGN PRODUCTION MANAGER Gavin Gibson
LITERARY MANAGER Jack Bradley
PLANNING PROJECT MANAGER Paul Jozefowski
RESIDENT DIRECTOR – LOFT Paul Miller
PRODUCTION CO-ORDINATOR Katrina Gilroy
PRODUCTION MANAGER – LOFT REALISATION Jo Maund
PRODUCTION ASSISTANTS – LOFT REALISATION Alan Bain, Gavin Gibson
LOFT LIGHTING REALISATION & TECHNICIANS Mike Atkinson, Steve Barnett,
    Pete Bull, Huw Llewellyn, Cat Silver
LOFT SOUND REALISATION Adam Rudd, Rich Walsh
LOFT STAGE TECHNICIANS Danny O'Neill, Stuart Smith
MODEL MAKERS Aaron Marsden, Riette Hayes-Davies
GRAPHIC DESIGNERS Patrick Eley, Stephen Cummiskey
PROGRAMME EDITOR Dinah Wood
PRESS Lucinda Morrison, Mary Parker, Gemma Gibb
MARKETING David Hamilton-Peters
PRODUCTION PHOTOGRAPHER Sheila Burnett

Thanks to the following people who were part of the original Lyttelton Development Group: Ushi Bagga, Alice Dunne, Annie Eves-Boland, Jonathan Holloway, Gareth James, Mark Jonathan, Holly Kendrick, Paul Jozefowski, Angus MacKechnie, Tim Redfern, Chris Shutt, Matt Strevens, Jane Suffling, Nicola Wilson, Dinah Wood, Lucy Woollatt

The National's workshops are responsible for, on these productions:
Armoury; Costume; Props & furniture; Scenic construction; Scenic Painting; Wigs

TRANSFORMATION SEASON

IN THE LYTTELTON

A co-production between the National Theatre & Théâtre National de Chaillot

The PowerBook . . . . 9 May–4 June
from a novel by Jeanette Winterson
devised by Jeanette Winterson, Deborah Warner & Fiona Shaw
Director Deborah Warner

A Prayer for Owen Meany . . . . 10–29 June
a novel by John Irving
adapted by Simon Bent
Director Mick Gordon

A collaboration between the National Theatre & Trestle Theatre Company

The Adventures of the Stoneheads . . . . 4–13 July
written & directed by Toby Wilsher

A collaboration between the National Theatre & Mamaloucos Circus

The Birds . . . . 23 July–3 August
by Aristophanes, in a new verse version by Sean O'Brien
Director Kathryn Hunter

Play Without Words . . . . 20 August–14 September
devised & directed by Matthew Bourne

IN THE LOFT

Sing Yer Heart Out for the Lads . . . . 29 April–15 May
by Roy Williams
Director Simon Usher

Free . . . . 20 May–8 June
by Simon Bowen
Director Thea Sharrock

Life After Life . . . . 28 May–8 June
a reportage play by Paul Jepson & Tony Parker
Director Paul Jepson

The Shadow of a Boy . . . . 13–29 June
by Gary Owen
Director Erica Whyman

The Mentalists . . . . 4–20 July
by Richard Bean
Director Sean Holmes

Sanctuary . . . . 25 July–10 August
by Tanika Gupta
Director Hettie Macdonald

The Associate . . . . 15–31 August
by Simon Bent
Director Paul Miller

Closing Time . . . . 4–21 September
by Owen McCafferty
Director James Kerr

NATIONAL THEATRE STUDIO &
TRANSFORMATION

All the plays in the LOFT are co-produced with the National Theatre Studio. The Studio is the National's laboratory for research and development, providing a workspace outside the confines of the rehearsal room and stage, where artists can experiment and develop their skills.

As part of its training for artists there is an on-going programme of classes, workshops, seminars, courses and masterclasses. Residencies have also been held in Edinburgh, Vilnius, Belfast and South Africa, enabling artists from a wider community to share and exchange experiences.

Central to the Studio's work is a commitment to new writing. The development and support of writers is demonstrated through play readings, workshops, short-term attachments, bursaries and sessions with senior writers. Work developed there continually reaches audiences throughout the country and overseas, on radio, film and television as well as at the National and other theatres. Most recent work includes the award-winning plays *Further than the Furthest Thing* by Zinnie Harris (Tron Theatre, Glasgow; Traverse, Edinburgh, and NT), *The Waiting Room* by Tanika Gupta (NT) and *Gagarin Way* by Gregory Burke (in association with Traverse, Edinburgh; NT; and at the Arts Theatre), *The Walls* by Colin Teevan (NT), *Accomplices* by Simon Bent, *Mr England* by Richard Bean (in association with Sheffield Theatres) and *The Slight Witch* by Paul Lucas (in association with Birmingham Rep), as well as a season of five new plays from around the world with the Gate Theatre, and *Missing Reel* by Toby Jones at the Traverse during the Edinburgh Festival 2001. *Gagarin Way* and *Further than the Furthest Thing* were part of SPRINGBOARDS – a series of partnerships created by the Royal National Theatre Studio with other theatres, enabling work by emerging writers to reach a wider audience.

Direct Action, a collaboration between The Studio and the Young Vic, is an initiative that provides young directors with an opportunity to work on the main stage of the Young Vic. Two plays were co-produced in the autumn of 2001: Max Frisch's *Andorra*, directed by Gregory Thompson; and David Rudkin's *Afore Night Come*, directed by Rufus Norris, who won the Evening Standard award for Best Newcomer for this production.

For the Royal National Theatre Studio

HEAD OF STUDIO	Sue Higginson
STUDIO MANAGER	Matt Strevens
TECHNICAL MANAGER	Eddie Keogh
INTERNATIONAL PROJECTS MANAGER	Philippe Le Moine
RESIDENT DIRECTOR (LOFT)	Paul Miller

Royal National Theatre
South Bank, London SE1 9PX
Box Office: 020 7452 3000
Information: 020 7452 3400

Registered Charity No: 224223

The chief aims of the National, under the direction of Trevor Nunn, are to present a diverse repertoire, embracing classic, new and neglected plays; to present these plays to the very highest standards; and to give audiences a wide choice.

All kinds of other events and services are on offer – short early-evening Platform performances; work for children and education work; free live entertainment both inside and outdoors at holiday times; exhibitions; live foyer music; backstage tours; bookshops; plenty of places to eat and drink; and easy car-parking. The nearby Studio acts as a resource for research and development for actors, writers and directors.

We send productions on tour, both in this country and abroad, and do all we can, through ticket-pricing, to make the NT accessible to everyone.

The National's home on the South Bank, opened in 1976, contains three separate theatres: the Olivier, the Lyttelton, and the Cottesloe and – during *Transformation* – a fourth: the Loft. It is open to the public all day, six days a week, fifty-two weeks a year. Stage by Stage – an exhibition on the NT's history, can be seen in the Olivier Gallery.

First published in 2002 by Oberon Books Ltd.
(incorporating Absolute Classics)
521 Caledonian Road, London N7 9RH
Tel: 020 7607 3637 / Fax: 020 7607 3629

e-mail: oberon.books@btinternet.com

A catalogue record for this book is available from the British
Library.

ISBN: 1 84002 278 7

Printed in Great Britain by Antony Rowe Ltd., Chippenham.

Characters

WATSON

RAY

TINY

Set in the present

The front room of a large Victorian house in West London, with two entrances, one leading to the hall and front door, the other to the kitchen, out back and the garage

Note

The following script was correct at the time of going to press but may differ slightly from the play as performed.

ACT ONE

Scene 1

Front room of Victorian terraced house. Floorboards, carpet up, old peeling wallpaper, pots of paint, buckets, step-ladders, brushes, rollers, painting and decorating materials. In the middle of the room WATSON, RAY and TINY sat at a table eating roast dinner with a bottle of red wine; TINY and RAY in overalls. RAY has finished eating. Night outside, curtains half-drawn. A radio on a chair to one side. During the scene night turns to day.

RAY: It's not safe, the world is not a safe place.

WATSON: No.

Silence.

TINY pushes plate away.

TINY: That's me done for.

WATSON: Bloody amateurs.

RAY: Terrorists.

TINY: I'm stuffed.

RAY: It nearly blew a woman's ears out in Bridge Avenue.

WATSON: More chicken.

TINY: No, I couldn't.

RAY: They could feel the blast seven miles away.

TINY: Alright, go on then.

TINY passes his plate to RAY who passes it on to WATSON.

RAY: I mean, what right – what right have they got, what right has anyone got to go round planting bombs and killing people.

WATSON: Breast or leg.

TINY: Breast.

RAY: It's like these anti-abortionists that go round shooting doctors, it's mad it doesn't make sense.

TINY: I do like a bit of breast.

WATSON passes plate to RAY who passes it to TINY.

RAY: Don't get me wrong, I'm not for abortion, I'm not anti-abortion, I don't know what I am, I'm not anything – I just don't think that anyone's got the right to kill anyone else.

WATSON: They should blow up the BBC.

TINY: I think that all nice people should be allowed to carry guns.

WATSON: Go on, have some chicken.

RAY: No, really, I can't, I don't – thanks.

WATSON: It's not natural, it's anti-social.

RAY: I don't mind other people eating meat, it's not moral.

TINY: No, it's his wife.

RAY: We're not married.

WATSON: It's not natural.

Silence.

The birds. You make it as far as the birds and you're safe.

TINY and WATSON carry on eating.

Silence.

RAY: How did you do the mash.

WATSON: With an unborn chicken, I put an egg in it.

RAY: Nice, very nice.

WATSON finishes eating, sits back and takes a drink.

WATSON: In five hundred years time, looking back, what do you think will be the defining moment of the twentieth century.

RAY: Oh.

TINY: Television.

WATSON: No.

RAY: The holocaust.

WATSON: No. Electricity. It's more important than the wheel, it's like fire – it is fire, it's the fire of the twentieth century.

RAY: Yeah.

TINY: What about the atomic bomb.

WATSON: Impossible without electricity. The modern world is electricity.

Raises glass.

Electricity.

RAY/TINY: (*Together.*) Electricity.

They all drink.

WATSON: I'm a reductionist.

TINY: My father's father was Jewish, what does that make me.

RAY: Tight.

WATSON: When my grandmother died they found every electricity bill she'd ever had since 1947 stuffed in a shoe box.

RAY: What did you do with them.

WATSON: Burnt them.

TINY: I'd have had them framed.

RAY: What for.

TINY: A souvenir.

WATSON: She didn't believe in banks she kept all her money at home under the floorboards, stuffed in socks, in the mattress, all in notes and all with her name written on them.

RAY: What did she write on them for.

WATSON: Because uncle Billy was doing the same thing. I don't believe in banks.

RAY: It must run in the family.

WATSON: Money, why is it that when anything's got anything to do with making money people think it's got something to do with intelligence.

RAY: I don't know.

WATSON: People are animals.

RAY: It's a big house. You've got a big house. It's big for council.

WATSON: My wife died.

RAY: Oh, I'm sorry.

TINY: What's for pudding.

WATSON: Dogs sort out their own politics – you take a pack of huskies, all you've got to do is harness their power and they do the rest – budge out the way I'm top dog.

TINY: We're not having any pudding then.

RAY: No.

WATSON: We started the Industrial Revolution, we were top dogs.

RAY: I'll clear the table.

WATSON: They wouldn't believe it, not even if they could see it with their own eyes, it's beyond belief we've sunk so low.

RAY: Pass me your plate.

TINY: Is that dinner done with then mister Watson.

RAY: Just pass me your plate.

TINY gives plate to RAY.

WATSON: My wife never forgave me.

TINY: What for.

WATSON: Everything.

WATSON gives his plate to RAY.

RAY: Thank you. I'll put these in the kitchen.

Exit RAY with plates.

TINY: He's worried about the council coming round.

WATSON: You're not brothers.

TINY: No.

Silence.

You've got a lot of butane gas cylinders and old alarm clocks in your garage mister Watson.

WATSON: Yes. I like mending broken clocks. I don't want you going in my garage without my say-so.

TINY: No, I didn't go in, I had a look through the window. And lots of fireworks.

WATSON: You look like brothers.

TINY: Like yeah, he's ugly. You want to be careful or you might blow yourself up.

WATSON: It's old stock.

TINY: Old stock.

WATSON: I had a sweet shop.

TINY: Have you got any sweets left.

WATSON: No.

TINY: You ate them all.

WATSON: No, they got liquidated.

TINY: Oh.

WATSON: I was bankrupted by the bank. They reneged on a loan. They gave me their word and then asked for their money back. Never trust the word of a bank manager.

TINY: No, I won't.

WATSON: Have another drink.

Fills their glasses.

Enter RAY with a bucket of warm water.

RAY: I'll mix up some sugar-soap.

Puts bucket down near wall.

TINY: Mister Watson had a sweet shop.

RAY: I used to dream about living in a sweet shop.

RAY opens packet of sugar soap.

WATSON: I was in concrete before that, and advertising before that – I sold a lot of concrete to the Nigerians in the seventies, I can sell anything. Cheers.

TINY: Cheers.

RAY: Cheers.

TINY and WATSON drink.

RAY tips sugar soap into bucket and stirs it in.

WATSON: We were top dogs, we civilised the world, and now people hug each other all the time and call each other mate.

TINY: We don't, we had a fight last week.

RAY: We had a disagreement.

TINY: It was a fight, we had a fight.

WATSON: Who won.

TINY: Cheeky.

WATSON: They hug you and smile and call you mate while they stab you in the back and take all your money – they've never done a day's work in their lives, they don't know what work is, nobody wants to work anymore.

RAY: I want to work.

TINY: I wouldn't work if I didn't have to.

RAY: Yes, but you have to.

TINY: If I won a million pounds I'd never hear another alarm clock again.

WATSON: It would deprive you of all ambition.

RAY: What ambition, he's got no ambition.

TINY: Yes I have.

RAY: What.

TINY: To win a million pounds.

RAY: I want to work, but they won't let you.

TINY: No, they won't mister Watson.

RAY: They won't – it's all Kosovans and Albanians and refugees – they get in on time, they cost less, they work all day, they don't take a break, they won't take a break, they just work, they'll do anything and they don't give a monkey's for safety.

TINY: They've got no expectations.

WATSON: It's over.

RAY: That's why I've gone self-employed, I've had to, to employ myself.

TINY: Yeah, nobody else would.

TINY drains wine bottle.

WATSON: It's all over, you've only got to look at the young to see that.

RAY: Right.

TINY: Yeah. There's a four and a half-year-old lives next door to me, he smokes all day and stays out till eleven o'clock at night.

WATSON: What does a four and a half-year-old find to do until eleven o'clock at night.

TINY: I don't know.

WATSON: He'll end up a murderer.

TINY: I'll open another bottle shall I.

RAY: I think we've all had enough.

WATSON: Five years ago this Wednesday my wife died.

TINY: I'll fetch another bottle.

RAY: Take some dishes with you.

TINY: Yes, boss.

Exit TINY with a dish.

Silence.

WATSON: You paint houses, for the council.

RAY: Yeah, you're our first contract.

Silence.

He's alright, we get on. He has his ways, I have mine – but when he goes off at ninety degrees he goes the full circle the full one hundred and eighty. You miss your wife.

WATSON: Married men die older than single men, they've got something to live for.

RAY: Someone to love.

WATSON: Somebody to hate.

RAY: We'll have this done in no time, it all just comes away –

Scrapes at wall with scraper and then pulls at paper tearing a huge strip off the wall.

See, easy.

WATSON: I have been hurt but not anymore I'm cold inside, women and children crying, you know – bits and pieces.

RAY: We've got a colour chart in the van.

WATSON: My days of hell-raising are over.

RAY: You've got a dark room under the stairs.

WATSON: You've got a van.

RAY: Yes, I'll move it if you want.

WATSON: No.

RAY: You develop your own pictures then.

WATSON: Yes, it's a hobby.

RAY: So, what do you take pictures of.

WATSON: People. I like your van.

RAY: Thank you.

Enter TINY with bottle.

WATSON: Sit down and have a drink.

RAY: No, thanks.

WATSON: Have another drink.

TINY: Yeah, come on I've opened the bottle now.

WATSON: Enjoy yourself while you still can.

TINY: You see, you give out good vibes and look what you get back.

TINY fills WATSON's glass.

WATSON: I could borrow your van.

TINY fills his glass.

TINY: Just this bottle and then we'll start work, come on boss.

RAY: I'm not the boss. I'm not your boss.

TINY: Alright.

RAY: We're self-employed.

TINY: So, have another drink.

WATSON: Have another drink.

TINY: We'll make up for this later.

WATSON: Go on, I'll see you're alright.

RAY: No, yes, oh alright just the one.

WATSON: Good lad.

TINY fills RAY's glass.

I could borrow your van for the day and go to France. All I need is a driver.

TINY: Cheers, boss.

TINY knocks back wine in one and refills his glass.

We should have gone self-employed years ago.

Refills glass.

WATSON: Don't forget to pay your stamp.

TINY: What's that then, dad. You don't mind if I call you dad do you, he doesn't mind.

WATSON: Yes, I do.

TINY: Oh.

WATSON: National Insurance.

RAY: NI.

TINY: Not interested.

RAY: Not in my case.

WATSON: You have to be clever not to get caught.

TINY: They won't catch you then, will they dad – mister Watson.

WATSON: Not unless I want them to.

RAY: Why, what have you done.

WATSON: Nothing.

TINY: This is the life, things are definitely looking up.

WATSON: We all have a moral obligation to live life to its full, and in this I have failed spectacularly.

RAY: You're not dead yet.

TINY: Who says.

RAY: You've got a tattoo on your arm mister Watson.

WATSON: Yes.

RAY: What's it say.

WATSON: Death before dishonour.

RAY: Nice.

WATSON: How big is your van.

RAY: Big enough.

TINY: You want to get yourself a girlfriend, mister Watson.

RAY: Like you you mean.

TINY: I'll ask her, I'm asking her.

WATSON: I wouldn't know where to start.

RAY: He fancies the Spanish bird in your deli.

WATSON: Yes she's nice.

RAY: But he's too shy to ask her out.

TINY: No, I'm not.

RAY: He's shy.

TINY: I'm not shy.

RAY: Shy boy.

WATSON: I've never had much luck with women.

TINY: You should go to Russia. The women are beautiful, they're big, they've got great posture and they wear loads of make up.

RAY: You've never been to Russia.

TINY: Tonight I'm going to meet a mad woman the maddest of all mad women and take her home and we'll have a drink and then she'll go into my bedroom and lie down on my bed and wait for me, and I'll make her wait.

WATSON: And then what.

TINY: I'll ask her what she wants.

WATSON: What does she want.

TINY: You know what she wants.

WATSON: What's her name.

TINY: Wendy.

RAY: Flipping heck.

TINY: Just ignore him, pop – mister Watson.

WATSON: What's Wendy wearing.

TINY: What do you think she's wearing.

RAY: Pyjamas.

WATSON: No, I can't do this.

TINY: Women, it's like a football match mister Watson – pumping balls down the middle all the time and getting nowhere – so get out on the wing mate, what you've got to do is get out on the wing, women are mad for it.

RAY: Yeah.

WATSON: No one wears pyjamas anymore.

TINY: How do you know.

WATSON: Because they don't.

TINY: He wears pyjamas.

RAY: No, I don't.

TINY: Yes you do.

RAY: I haven't got any pyjamas.

TINY: He wears his wife's pyjamas.

RAY: No, I don't.

TINY: Big girl's pyjamas.

RAY: She's not my wife, we never got married.

TINY: You had a baby.

RAY: I don't wear her pyjamas.

TINY: You get back with her and I'm filing for a divorce.

RAY: I live with someone else.

TINY: You still fancy her.

RAY: I don't.

TINY: You want her back.

RAY: I don't, I don't want to get back with her; how can I get back with her when we don't even talk, she hates my guts.

TINY: You still want her.

RAY: I live with another woman.

TINY: You want her.

RAY: No I don't.

TINY: Yes you do.

RAY: I don't.

TINY: You do.

RAY: I don't.

TINY: You want her.

RAY: I don't want to fuck her, alright.

Silence.

WATSON: Have another drink.

RAY: I'm sorry about that mister Watson.

Fills RAY's glass.

TINY: It's his ex-wife.

RAY: We never got married.

TINY gets up from table.

TINY: Here, watch this, you'll like this –

RAY: I'll go and get the colour chart.

TINY: No, no, you'll like it I promise – this is me going down the stairs right –

Mimes walking down behind table.

And this is me going down in a lift.

Mimes pushing a button and descends from knees behind table.

Do you get it, it's good isn't it.

RAY: Yeah, yeah. Can I have a cup of coffee, please.

TINY: Finish your drink, have another drink – he knows, you know, mister Watson –

WATSON: Stanley.

TINY: Stanley knows – Stanley?

WATSON: Stanley Grosvenor Watson. I was named after the restauraunt I was conceived in.

TINY: Stanley's.

WATSON: The Grosvenor Steak Bar. My mother was a waitress and my father was the chef. I was a source of deep regret for both of them.

TINY: Stanley knows we'll catch up, don't you Stanley.

WATSON: He ran off with a pastry cook shortly after I was born.

RAY: She's taken me for every penny I've got and more, I won't lie down and die. Bitch.

RAY drinks.

I'm a good working-class lad, my dad said if you haven't got it in your pocket then you can't spend it – I've never been in debt in my life.

TINY: She's not worth it.

RAY: I know she's not worth it.

TINY: The only reason why people like her, right – is because she's blonde, she's small, she's pretty, and she's very, very – not very nice – that's all she is, blonde, pretty, and – it's not worth it.

RAY: I owe the bank two thousand pounds.

TINY: She had your baby.

WATSON: You could drive me to France in your van.

TINY: I nearly had a baby, but she miscarried after three weeks. It made us closer. Have you ever had a miscarriage Stanley.

WATSON: No. But my wife did, with another man.

TINY: I felt this overwhelming sense of responsibility.

RAY: You've never felt that before.

TINY: No. And then I left her.

WATSON: We never had children.

TINY: I'm what you call a rough cut diamond.

Pours everyone a drink.

WATSON: My wife drove me mad, she kept me awake at night with her nagging and her snoring, reading and sucking on mints – until finally I snapped, I put a pillow over her face and tried to smother her. I'd been trying to sleep for years. She stopped talking after that. It started off with a couple of days and then two days became two months and two months two years, then the next thing I heard her say was, 'I'm leaving you.' I woke up the next morning and found her hanging from the bannister, and a note on the hallstand saying, 'The strain of it all was too much.'

Silence.

On her sixtieth birthday she got a letter from the
Department of Social Security informing her that she
was no longer eligible for a pension due to the fact that
she was dead.

RAY: I'll put this chicken in the kitchen.

Exit RAY with chicken.

Silence.

TINY: It'll look nice when it's all finished. Have you
decided what colour yet.

WATSON: White.

TINY: Nice, very nice. Won't be long now.

Silence.

They've proved that lesbians have a tendency to go
deaf.

WATSON: Do you drive.

TINY: Yeah I do, I can, I haven't got a licence, but I don't.

WATSON: You're no good.

TINY: Thanks a bunch Stanley.

Enter RAY.

RAY: Right, that's the lot.

WATSON: Have another drink Raymond.

RAY: No, really Mr Watson.

WATSON: Stanley.

RAY: Stanley.

WATSON: Don't worry about the council, I'm thinking of writing them a letter.

RAY: Oh, yeah.

WATSON: Yes.

RAY sits and WATSON pours him a drink.

TINY: I've successfully separated my love life and sex life.

WATSON: So, you just have sex.

TINY: Yeah.

WATSON: What do you have.

TINY: He gets nothing, he's married.

RAY: We live together.

TINY: And you sleep with her in your ex–wife's pyjamas.

RAY: We never got married.

WATSON: You should have sex with a girl tonight and then tell me about it tomorrow.

TINY: I should have sex with a girl tonight and not tell you about it.

WATSON: Oh, no, that would be mean.

TINY: Live dangerously, grandad – take your socks off.

RAY: What are you going to say in this letter.

WATSON: How would you like to drive me to France for the day, in your van.

RAY: What for.

WATSON: To get some wine.

Doorbell rings.

RAY: Who's that.

WATSON: I don't know.

TINY: Don't look at me.

Silence.

RAY: It's the council.

TINY: No, it's not.

RAY: Who normally calls round this time of day.

WATSON: Nobody.

Silence.

RAY: Look out the window.

TINY: I'm not looking out the window.

RAY: Maybe they'll go away.

Doorbell rings.

WATSON: No they won't. We'll go by ferry, I'm not going in that tunnel, you won't catch me in any tunnel; that's what they should blow up, that and the BBC.

Exit WATSON.

RAY: It is, it's the council.

TINY: No it's not, they're all in bed.

RAY removes his chair and WATSON's from the table and stacks them out of the way. Comes back for TINY's chair. TINY doesn't move.

RAY: Move will you.

TINY remains seated.

Just move.

TINY stands and RAY takes his chair away.

Open a tin of paint.

TINY: What for.

RAY: Open a tin of paint.

TINY: I'm clearing the table.

TINY finishes the remains of each glass. As he does RAY picks up the empty glasses and bottle.

RAY: Open a tin of paint.

Exit RAY.

TINY turns on radio. Music. Sits on a chair and reads paper. Enter RAY with bucket of water and two large yellow sponges.

TINY: 'West London in letter bomb terror,' it's all going on in this neck of the woods. The IRA blowing up bridges and this madman.

RAY turns off radio.

One to a supermarket and the other to a bank.

RAY takes one end of the table.

RAY: Help me with this.

TINY: Demanding huge amounts of money.

RAY: Move will you.

TINY: Alright.

*They move table to one side and cover it with dust sheet.
RAY starts to wet wall with sponge and sugar soap*

RAY: You're not going to fuck this up for me, you fuck this up for me Tiny and I'll tie a knot in your cock so tight that you'll wish you'd never been born.

TINY: You're stressing man, stop stressing.

RAY: I'm not stressing.

TINY: You are.

RAY: I'm not.

TINY: You're stressed.

RAY: I'm not stressed, alright.

TINY: Alright. Calm, calm.

Enter WATSON wearing an old overcoat loose, gloves, a camera round his neck and a thick black book in hand. TINY has his back to him.

You want to watch it mate or you'll end up like Stanley.

RAY: Mister Watson – we, we're just getting started, who was that at the door.

WATSON: The milkman.

RAY: Is that a Bible.

WATSON: I'll open the curtains.

TINY: No, I'll do it.

RAY: So, you're a Christian.

Curtains open. Daylight.

WATSON: No.

RAY: But you're reading the Bible.

WATSON: Yes.

TINY: Where have you got up to.

WATSON: The suffering of Job.

TINY: Right.

WATSON: I know Psalm 24 by heart.

RAY: Is that famous then.

WATSON: No, that's Psalm 23.

RAY: Oh.

WATSON: I learnt it while I was on a mission ship in North Africa – we went round ministering to the needs of the sick and the poor, I was responsible for organising the entertainments – we were involved in spiritual warfare – it was our responsibility to go into areas of dark satanic influence and spread the word of God – we'd do a bit of mime, song and dance – people got very hostile.

TINY: Did you do any juggling.

WATSON: Not personally, no.

RAY: How did you know where to go.

WATSON: God told us. He sent us to Northern Iraq, Turkey – the ship was called the Anastasis. That's Greek for resurrection.

RAY: It'll be the juggling that put people off.

TINY: Job, he got swallowed by the whale.

WATSON: No, that was Jonah.

TINY: That's him. Imagine being swallowed by a whale.

RAY: You'd probably get stuck in it's throat.

TINY: No, imagine being stuck in the belly of a whale.

RAY: What for.

TINY: The story of Jonah.

RAY: Pinnochio and his dad.

WATSON: We live in the belly of the whale and there is no light.

Silence.

RAY: You don't believe in God anymore.

WATSON: No, it's all a matter of simple sexual desire, procreation, and when that's done we're left with this husk and an aberration called consciousness waiting to die.

Silence.

TINY: It's a bit blooming bleak, isn't it. What about fun, you know fun, having a bit of fun.

Looks at RAY and WATSON.

They look back at him blankly.

Silence.

No.

WATSON: The last thing I see when I die will be the end of my nose.

RAY: You've decided then.

WATSON: It will.

RAY: What if you're blind.

TINY: You're such a bloody pessimist – sorry about the French Stanley – but he is, you are, the glass is always half empty.

WATSON: I'll leave this here for you to read.

WATSON places Bible on table.

TINY: We're all descended from swimming apes.

RAY: Speak for yourself.

RAY wets wall with sponge and starts to scrape off paper. TINY picks up wallpaper scraper.

TINY: I used to think that UFOs, right, were from another planet, another universe, a distant solar system – and then I got to thinking, why don't they ever attack?

RAY: We don't want to know, alright.

TINY: Alright.

RAY and TINY begin stripping the wall and continue to do so to the end of the scene.

WATSON: I have to go out.

RAY: You go out, don't worry about us mister Watson.

WATSON: I'm not.

RAY: You go out, we're alright.

WATSON: I've got some packages to deliver and a letter to post.

TINY: Because they're from the future man, that's where we come from, that's why they don't attack.

WATSON: A Godless world in which they'll be able to do what they want with us, clone us, put microchips in us, control us – they can already tell what parts of the brain are thinking what by scanning it. I've had it done, I've had my brain photographed. They put me in a machine.

RAY: What for.

WATSON: I had a stroke.

RAY: (*To TINY.*) Just work will you.

TINY: I'm working.

RAY: But you're alright now, mister Watson.

WATSON: I'm alright, I'm always alright, it's other people that aren't alright.

RAY: You want to look after yourself.

WATSON: I do.

TINY: I'm working, alright. Get plenty of fresh air and exercise Stanley.

WATSON: That didn't do next door much good. He bought weights and started jogging.

TINY: What happened.

WATSON: He choked to death on a vitamin tablet.

TINY: I take vitamins.

RAY: Yeah, of the chemical variety, and the last time they had to call out an ambulance and rush you to hospital.

TINY: It was the strichnyne, they had strichnyne in them – it wasn't the vitamins.

WATSON: I have to go to the supermarket and the bank.

RAY: You don't like banks.

WATSON: You drive me to France in your van to get some wine and I'll write you a letter to the council saying what a good job you're doing.

RAY: You just say the word chief.

WATSON: I will.

TINY: You're going to take some photographs.

WATSON: Hopefully. I've got a letter to post and some packages to deliver first.

RAY: You be careful, it's not safe out there, the world is not a safe place.

Exit WATSON.

TINY: He's off his fucking trolley.

RAY: Yeah, but he's prepared to write us a good reference.

TINY: Who in their right mind has Sunday dinner for breakfast.

RAY: Just fucking humour him, alright.

TINY: Yeah, alright.

RAY turns on radio. Pop music.

RAY: I'll put the kettle on.

TINY: Fuck that, I'm going down the shop to get a beer. Do you want anything.

RAY: No, no – oh alright, Special Brew.

Exit TINY.

RAY stands staring at the wall. Light fades.

Scene 2

Front room. Day. The walls half stripped bare. Step-ladders. RAY stripping the wall. Radio on, playing classical music.

Enter TINY with carrier bag. Retunes radio to pop.

RAY: I was listening to that.

TINY slumps against a wall. RAY goes to radio.

TINY: Leave it.

RAY turns off radio.

You should've been a vicar. He's not back yet then.

RAY: No.

TINY: That's lucky, we'll say we got in at nine-thirty then.

RAY: No, ten.

TINY: Nine o'clock even.

RAY: Just after ten.

TINY: Yeah, but if we get in at nine and don't have lunch we're into overtime at five.

RAY: We don't get overtime.

TINY: Oh yeah – so we knock off early then.

TINY opens can of lager.

RAY: What did you get.

TINY: Packet of crisps, extra strong lager, bar of chocolate and a sausage roll.

RAY: You've got everything you need to be happy there.

TINY: Happiness in a bag, d'you want some.

RAY: No.

TINY: No, you wouldn't. He doesn't care, it doesn't matter to him what time we get here, he's not paying the council are paying.

RAY: I don't like being late.

TINY: Don't look at me, I didn't make us late, it's not my fault I have to sign on at ten-thirty. What do you want me to do.

RAY: Stop signing on.

TINY: You stop signing on.

RAY: Yeah, I might.

TINY: Yeah.

TINY opens chocolate.

RAY: You're not working.

TINY: I'm having breakfast.

RAY: It's nearly dinner.

TINY: I haven't had any breakfast.

RAY: We'll say we got here just after ten.

TINY: He's making some sort of thing out in the garage – about this big, metal tube and wires sticking out of it.

RAY: Keep out of that garage.

TINY: I never went in.

RAY: He said to keep out.

TINY: He's put a padlock on the door.

RAY: Just keep out.

TINY: I never went in, alright.

RAY: This is the gravy train it's pulled into my station and I'm jumping on, you're not going to fuck it up for me, alright.

TINY: I looked through the window.

RAY: You're a nosey bugger you.

TINY: Somebody locks a door and you wonder why.

RAY: No, I don't.

TINY: No, you wouldn't.

TINY picks up scraper.

RAY: Bloody hell Tiny, are you feeling alright.

TINY: I work.

TINY scrapes wall.

But what do you think he does in there all day, what do you think he's doing.

RAY: Making alterations to the Time Machine.

TINY: Just grow up will you.

RAY: Like you, you mean.

TINY: Yeah.

RAY: Plank.

TINY: It's not me that's a plank, you're the plank.

RAY: How was your girlfriend.

TINY: No, I went to the Paki's.

RAY: Liar.

TINY: I just like her that's all – she's very, very – you know, Spanish – fuck off.

RAY: Ask her out.

TINY: I will.

RAY: No, you won't.

TINY: I will.

RAY: I'll ask her for you if you like.

TINY: How's your ex-wife.

RAY: I will, I'll ask her for you.

TINY: And I'll go round and shag your ex-wife for you.

RAY: We never got married and you're welcome to her.

TINY: She's got a new boyfriend.

RAY: It's got nothing to do with me.

TINY: Apparently he's in training to be a Buddhist monk.

RAY: I don't know.

TINY: They met while praying for World peace.

RAY: Where's the office. Where have you put the office.

TINY: Drives a flash motor.

RAY: I can't find the office.

RAY turns on radio: pop music.

What have you done with the office, Tiny.

TINY: Nothing. Twenty-six and he's loaded.

RAY: You had it last.

TINY: No I didn't.

RAY: You did.

TINY: I didn't.

RAY: You had it in the van, I asked you to bring it in with you.

TINY: No you never.

RAY: I told you to bring it in.

TINY: You never.

RAY: I did.

TINY: You never.

RAY: Where have you put the office Tiny, what have you done with the office.

TINY: Nothing, I haven't done anything with the office.

RAY: You can't do anything can you, I have to do everything, why is it always me, why is it always down to me, on my shoulders my responsibility – well I've had enough, I've had it up to here – don't you laugh at me, don't you dare laugh at me –

TINY: I'm not, it's not me that's laughing.

RAY: I carry you pal, I've always carried you – and you don't know when to stop, you never know when to stop – you just take take take, you're taking the piss, and it's never enough – well that's it, I've had it, I wash my hands – I've given enough, I've done enough, you've taken enough – you're on your own, not anymore – see how you like it on your own.

TINY: All I said was, 'How's your ex-wife?'

RAY: Arrrrrrgh!

Kicks over the step-ladders. Music stops.

She's not my wife we never got married I don't care I'm not interested –

Enter WATSON with passport and large brown envelope.

WATSON: What's all the racket for.

RAY: Mister Watson.

TINY: Stanley.

WATSON: Don't you Stanley me.

TINY: We were just stopping for a break and the ladders fell over.

RAY: Yeah, they fell over.

RAY picks up ladders.

WATSON: When did you two get here.

TINY: (*Simultaneous with RAY.*) Nine o'clock.

RAY: (*Simultaneous with TINY.*) Just after ten.

TINY: I'll go and have a look for the office.

Exit TINY.

WATSON: You're late.

RAY: We broke down.

WATSON: Where's he gone.

RAY: To get the office.

WATSON: He'll be down the shop, he's always going down the shop.

RAY: We thought you'd gone out.

WATSON: Sniffing round her Spanish hemline.

RAY: You haven't been out.

WATSON: No, the weather stopped me.

RAY: Right.

WATSON: I gave your dinner to next door's dog.

RAY: It won't happen again.

WATSON: I'm not cooking you dinner again.

RAY: I'm sorry mister Watson there was nothing we could do the van broke down and we had to wait.

WATSON: You'll be here till Christmas.

RAY: We'll get it done.

WATSON: I could ring the council.

RAY: No, we're further on than it looks chief – it's all about preparation there's no point rushing you can't rush quality work.

WATSON: I'm not going to France in a van that breaks down all the time.

RAY: No it's alright, that was just this morning, we had it fixed there's nothing wrong with it now.

WATSON: I know what you're up to.

RAY: Goes like a rocket.

WATSON: I should ring the council.

Enter TINY with small battered brown suitcase.

TINY: Catch.

Throws suitcase to RAY unprepared. RAY catches it.

And may it bring you much happiness.

WATSON: What's that.

TINY: His office.

RAY: I was just saying how the van broke down.

TINY: Well open it then. You're not going to open it.

RAY: No.

WATSON: You were late.

TINY: The van broke down Stanley, and we got stuck in traffic.

RAY: Yeah – yes, we did, the police have closed off Hammersmith roundabout because of a bomb scare in Tesco's, an old lady took a bomb home with her in a shopping bag.

WATSON: I know what your game is.

TINY: Oh, yeah.

WATSON: Yes, you can't kid a kidder.

TINY: I'm not with you, dad.

WATSON: And I'm not your dad.

TINY: I went and got the office for nothing then.

RAY: The old woman's gone into a coma – it was the shock, she had a history of epilepsy and it started her off, they reckon she might never recover. If she dies it'll be murder.

WATSON: What for.

RAY: He's killed her, it's the bombers fault.

WATSON: He didn't intend to kill her.

RAY: He planted a bomb, he didn't care who got killed.

WATSON: Yes – but it wasn't his intention to kill that old lady in particular, surely not.

RAY: No, he's callous.

WATSON: You think so.

RAY: He doesn't care who he maims or kills just as long as he gets what he wants.

WATSON: We don't know what he wants.

RAY: Yes we do, money.

RAY picks up newspaper.

TINY: Yeah, he wants the banks and the supermarkets to fork out shedloads of it.

WATSON: Yes, but to what end.

TINY: To buy things with, Stanley.

RAY: Here it is, he's written a letter to the papers, (*Reads.*) 'The Association is a small but virulent group of consumer victims, our manifesto is to stem the tidal wave of consumerism and to burn a hole in the pocket of corporate capitalism by making it pay out huge amounts of money. We have the will we have the ability we have access to a constant supply of explosive materials. Meet our demands or suffer the consequences. The public is not our enemy. You have one week's grace, Yours sincerely, The Associate Bomber.'

WATSON: Clearly written by a man of high moral principle and a flair for public relations.

TINY: And he's a paedophile.

WATSON: No, he's not.

TINY: Yes, he is.

WATSON: Why would he be – this man's clever, sophisticated, running a military-style operation, he's a strategist, a fox, he only strikes intermittently and after long periods of silence.

TINY: Yeah, he's a paedophile.

RAY: You seem to know a lot about it mister Watson.

WATSON: Yes, I've been following it in the news.

TINY: I'd hang them all, terrorists, bombers, rapists, perverts, paedophiles, the lot, and castrate them.

WATSON: You've got no compassion.

TINY: I've got no compassion, I haven't raped anyone.

WATSON: Neither has he.

TINY: And I don't mean chemical castration either.

WATSON: That's why we've got laws, to protect people from people like you.

RAY: That old lady hadn't done him any harm, all she was doing was her shopping, what harm had she done.

WATSON: The shop should have taken precautions. They should have put out warnings, maybe even paid off the bomber.

TINY: Yeah, and then everybody starts planting bombs and asking for money.

WATSON: No, it takes a special kind of personality.

RAY: But what wrong had she done him.

WATSON: Nothing. It's not personal, this has got nothing to do with personalities. It's the same in any war.

RAY: But this isn't a war.

WATSON: No, but it is for the bomber. The government and the supermarket should have done more, they should never have put an old lady at risk like that – they're as much to blame for this as the bomber – but they won't accept responsibilty, they'll lie their way out of it – people's scruples have gone down the drain nobody tells the truth anymore – they lie under oath, they cheat, they steal, nothing's sacred – it's after years of telling people to think only of themselves – I've a good mind to write to the prime minister about it, or the deputy prime minister; him and his Jags, what does he know.

TINY: I still say castrate him.

WATSON: It's preposterous, I don't see how the World can go on like this for much longer, do you?

RAY: No.

WATSON: It's all gone to pot, everything's falling apart, you've only got to look at the young.

TINY: I'm not falling apart.

RAY: No, he means the young. You're a girl.

Picks up wallpaper scraper.

He's the only bloke I know turns his head when he hears a wolf-whistle in the street mister Watson.

Returns to work.

TINY: Only to see what they're whistling at.

RAY: In case it's a woman whistling at him.

WATSON: I wake up early every morning and I have this feeling, a feeling of despair. And there's nothing I can do. And then the light comes and I get up.

TINY: I woke up early this morning on the floor naked with a sock in my hand and it was raining.

RAY: Obviously a good night out.

TINY: Yeah, it was.

WATSON: You met Wendy.

TINY: No

WATSON: She stood you up.

TINY: She doesn't exist, I made her up.

WATSON: Oh, I was looking forward to meeting her.

RAY: He went midnight shopping on Green Lanes, Stanley

TINY: I don't, not anymore, alright.

RAY: Alright.

TINY picks up scraper.

RAY and TINY work.

WATSON: For twenty years I drank in the same pub, I had the same job, I lived with the same woman...they were my friends, it was my job, she was my wife...and so it would go on...and nobody gave a damn. I don't go out, I stopped going out. I tried watching the television instead, but that's no good, the telly's no good, it's rubbish.

TINY: One Eyed Baz came in the pub looking for you.

RAY: What did you tell him.

TINY: Why, what have you done.

WATSON: The difference is that God appeared to Job, Job suffered and Job was rewarded.

Exit WATSON leaving passport and envelope on table.

RAY: So, what did One Eyed Baz say.

TINY: About what.

RAY: I don't know.

TINY: You owe him money.

RAY: No I don't.

TINY: You've borrowed money.

RAY: What do you think I am, stupid.

TINY: He'll break both your legs.

RAY: No, he won't.

TINY: He will.

RAY: I don't owe him anything.

TINY: Alright.

TINY goes over to table and picks up envelope.

RAY: That's not yours.

TINY: I know.

RAY: Put it down.

TINY: I'm having a look that's all.

Slides out large photographs.

RAY: What are they.

TINY: Photographs.

RAY: Put them back.

TINY: Photographs of people shopping.

Sound of pots and pans crashing to floor in kitchen.

TINY stuffs photographs in envelope and goes back to work.

Enter WATSON with bottle of wine and glass.

TINY and RAY work.

WATSON sits and pours a glass of wine.

Silence.

Drinks.

Cheer up dad, it might never happen.

WATSON: It already has.

WATSON drinks glass back in one and refills it.

RAY: Other people are never as happy as you think they are mister Watson.

TINY: Miserable sod.

RAY: It's true.

TINY: You are you're miserable.

TINY stops working.

We call him Smiler, Stanley.

WATSON: I'd never go out again if I didn't have to.

TINY: Because he smiles a lot.

RAY: I'll hit you.

WATSON: People falling over, drunk, fighting, in the middle of the night, drinking themselves insensible, to death. The world is in such a terrible state it's drowning itself in drink in order to forget. We should never forget. A land fit for heroes. And now they get mugged. We've all been mugged.

Refills glass.

I don't drink, I've given up drink.

TINY: What do you call that.

WATSON: Wine.

TINY: You're always going out.

WATSON: Because I have to.

TINY: No you don't, you're retired.

WATSON: There are things I have to do, I have to go out right to the bitter end – I don't mind dying, I'm not frightened of dying, why should I be.

TINY: You're not dying.

WATSON: Who says.

RAY: He used to be frightened of dogs, now it's just women mister Watson.

TINY: Watch it you.

RAY: Or what.

TINY: He wouldn't stand a chance Stanley.

TINY flicks water at him with sponge.

RAY: Behave.

WATSON: I was making a bacon sandwich and the four horsemen of the apocolypse came for me – they didn't want feeding they wanted my soul and a great gaping black hole opened up under my feet and I struggled to raise my voice my whole body straining to make a sound but I couldn't I had no voice.

Silence.

RAY: Maybe it was something you ate.

WATSON: I was dreaming and you woke me up.

RAY goes back to work.

Have a drink.

TINY: No, I can't.

WATSON: Come on, just the one. He's the worker, you're the brains of the outfit.

TINY: Oh, alright, I'll catch up later.

WATSON: Good lad.

TINY picks up an empty mug and WATSON fills it for him.

So, who's One Eyed Baz.

TINY: He's a big black mean looking bugger with a glass eye, drinks pints of cider with ice in it, drug-dealer, wears suits a lot, ugly, lends money, foreign.

WATSON: How do you know he's foreign.

TINY: He look's foreign.

RAY: He's not foreign.

TINY: He's half Spanish half Portuguese and half African, what's that make him.

RAY: Impossible.

WATSON: And he owes him money.

RAY: No.

WATSON: You're working.

RAY: Right you are, chief.

TINY: Let's have a look at your passport, I promise I won't laugh.

WATSON: It's for going to France with.

TINY picks up passport.

There was a butcher on the Broadway who only had one eye: a blood stained apron one mad staring eye and a meat cleaver in his hand. You won't get that in a supermarket.

RAY: No, no you won't.

WATSON: We don't have a butchers anymore, we don't have a fishmongers, we used to have an eel and pie shop – it's all supermarkets and coffee republics, bars with sofas and cushions on the floor, everywhere you look it's the set of an American situation-comedy about middle-aged young people acting like they're in a pop group.

TINY looks at passport.

TINY: You can't laugh at that Stanley, you look better in the photograph than you do in real life.

TINY lights a cigarette.

You look like an axe murderer. You should take some pictures of me I'm very very photogenetic.

Gives passport to WATSON.

WATSON: I have looked into the face of the world and I have seen such things, such things as I cannot speak of them.

TINY: What's in the envelope.

WATSON: Nothing.

TINY: It's not photographs then.

WATSON: No, why would it be.

TINY: No reason. When are we going to France.

WATSON: It's not decided.

RAY: It's nice of you to drop in like this, Tiny.

TINY: I'm having a fag and a drink with mister Watson.

WATSON: Find yourself a mug son.

TINY: Yeah, come on.

RAY: I want to finish this wall.

RAY continues working.

WATSON: You haven't got anyone special in your life.

TINY: No.

WATSON: What about the girl you nearly had a baby with.

TINY: I loved her Stanley, I really loved her but she wanted me to stop sleeping with other women.

WATSON: And you didn't.

TINY: You can't fight human nature Stanley; what was I meant to do, kill myself. It all got awkward when I slept with her sister, well not awkward but you know.

WATSON: It's another world.

TINY: She's got a fantastic body.

WATSON: Has she.

TINY: She has. All fleshy.

WATSON: Would I like her.

TINY: Yes, you would Stanley.

WATSON: Where does she live.

TINY: Sunderland.

WATSON: Oh.

RAY: How is she.

TINY: Good, yeah, she's good, she's seeing a psychiatrist.

WATSON: I once spent the night in Sunderland selling concrete.

TINY: She's like honey, a pot of wild honey you just want to keep on dipping into.

WATSON: I had a corned beaf and mashed potato and onion sandwich.

TINY: She's working on how to let go of her name.

WATSON: What for.

TINY: To get rid of her ego.

WATSON: I see.

RAY: Lend us your matches.

TINY throws box to RAY.

TINY: Maybe I could get her to come down and teach you how to let go of your name.

WATSON: Oh, I don't know about that.

RAY lights up.

TINY: She'd like you.

WATSON: Do you think so.

TINY: I do.

RAY: (*Reading matchbox.*) Going Places.

WATSON: Yes, the grave.

RAY throws matches back to TINY.

Sometimes I wake up and I don't know who I am, I forget names, I forget places, I suddenly find myself in a room and I don't know why I'm there.

TINY: Yeah, well –

RAY: That's you finished for the day is it.

TINY: Alright.

WATSON: They gave me a personality test.

TINY: Did you pass.

WATSON: I got the highest score for memory that they'd ever had.

TINY: So, they knew you then.

WATSON: No.

RAY: Don't mind me, you take as long as you want.

TINY: Alright, I'm coming. How can they test your memory if they don't know you.

WATSON: It's alright to look for hope in small things, but to look for it in anything else, to seek salvation…there is no salvation…

TINY: Show us your photographs.

WATSON: What photographs.

Silence.

WATSON pours himself a glass of wine.

TINY: I'd better get back to work.

WATSON: I've got something for you.

TINY: Oh, yeah.

WATSON: Yes, it was in the hall – I looked down and found it on the floor next to a pound.

TINY: See, things are looking up already, that's the thing to do Stanley, always look down.

WATSON holds out an unemployment benefit book.

WATSON: You'll need it for when you next sign on.

TINY takes book.

TINY: Oh, thank you – no, no, this is not for signing on with.

WATSON: It's a benefit book.

TINY: Yes, yes it is.

WATSON: And it's got your name on.

TINY: Yes, that is my name – but this is not for signing on with – I mean, I have used it to sign on with, but I don't, not anymore – this, this is an old one that I'm in the process of returning.

RAY: On what day again was it that you said you wanted to go to France mister Watson.

WATSON: I don't know, a complication has arisen with my supplier.

RAY: Oh, a complication.

WATSON: Yes, I'm in discussion with a new supplier.

TINY: What are you making in the garage.

WATSON: Nothing. I've got my eye on you, I know what's going on. I expect to arrive at a satisfatory deal very soon. (*Goes to exit.*) 'Honni soit qui mal y pense.'

Exit WATSON.

RAY: Pass me the office.

TINY throws suitcase to RAY. RAY opens suitcase and takes out a can of lager and closes suitcase. RAY opens can, drinks.

TINY: I didn't know, how was I to know – I didn't drop it on purpose.

RAY: You toy.

TINY: There's something going on that we don't know about.

RAY: There's a lot going on that we don't know about.

TINY: Yeah, more than we can think.

RAY: You are, you're a toy.

RAY picks up suitcsase.

TINY: Where are you going.

RAY: To do some office work.

TINY: I'll come with you.

RAY: No.

TINY: I'll get an office of my own then.

RAY: Yeah, you do that.

Exit RAY.

TINY: Ray, no don't go, Ray –

Jerks right fist in air while slapping down on the bicep with left hand.

To you as well, mate.

End of Act One.

ACT TWO

Scene 1

Front room, night. Walls completely stripped bare. Several wooden boxes of wine stacked on the floor. TINY on phone in corner of room.

TINY: Yeah, that's right…an eight o'clock appointment…
with Mistress Ilana… No, I can't – I've just got back
from France – I'm not paying a cancellation fee –

Enter RAY with box of wine.

You know my black jeans…see them, yeah…there's a
pound in one of the pockets, take it out – No you can't
spend it. Put it on the window sill. Yeah, yeah. I'll be
there as soon as I can.

TINY puts down phone. RAY stacks box.

It's my dad.

Silence.

He's coming to stop.

Silence.

RAY lights up a cigarette.

Give us a ciggy.

Silence.

How much longer are you going to keep this up for.

Silence.

I have to go.

RAY: We're not finished.

TINY: Oh, yes we are.

RAY: When this job's done that's when you're finished.

TINY: It's my dad.

RAY: I don't care what she calls herself.

TINY: I don't, not anymore, I've given all that up.

RAY: You can do what you like, I'm not your mother.

TINY: I don't like the French.

RAY: It's your money.

TINY: I don't like France, and I don't like the French.

RAY: You've only been to Calais for the day.

TINY: Yeah, and Calais is in France and it's full of French people.

RAY: Unload the van.

TINY: Fuck you.

TINY goes to exit. RAY grabs him by the jacket and draws him up close.

RAY: You're not going anywhere until we're finished.

TINY: Take your hands off me. I said get off.

RAY lets go.

I'll do what I want.

RAY: You'll do as I say.

TINY: Oh, yeah.

RAY: Yeah.

Silence.

TINY: Come on then.

Pause.

No, you couldn't.

RAY goes for TINY, knocks TINY into stack of boxes, knocking them to the floor. RAY and TINY fight on floor. Enter WATSON.

WATSON: You've left the van open.

RAY: Mister Watson.

TINY: Stanley.

WATSON: What are you doing.

RAY: We're having a break.

TINY: Yeah, a break.

RAY: And Tiny fell over.

TINY: I fell over.

RAY: And I was helping him to stand up.

TINY: Yeah…he was helping me to stand up –

TINY and RAY laugh.

WATSON: What are you laughing at.

RAY: Nothing.

TINY: No, it's not funny.

TINY and RAY laugh.

WATSON: Some of those boxes are worth over a thousand pounds.

TINY: How much.

RAY: That's nearly a hundred pounds a bottle.

WATSON: Look at you, no wonder the country's in such a state. Get that van unloaded and we'll open a bottle to celebrate.

TINY: What are we celebrating.

WATSON: Getting home.

Exit WATSON.

TINY: Scum.

RAY: He kept that quiet.

TINY: Typical scum, he doesn't trust us.

RAY: No.

TINY: No.

RAY: Three of those boxes would do me.

Both stare at boxes. Silence.

No.

TINY: No.

RAY: No, it's not enough. And he lives in a council house.

TINY: Ask no questions, know no answers that's what I say.

RAY: Your family motto. Nothing's changed.

TINY: I never said it had.

RAY: After this job I'm never working with you again.

RAY up-ends one of boxes knocked to floor.

TINY: If anything's broke you're paying for it, you can borrow it from One Eyed Baz – add it to what you owe him already. He's going to break your legs.

RAY: No, he's not.

TINY: And I'll pay to watch.

RAY: I don't owe him anything.

TINY: Two and a half grand.

RAY: How do you know.

TINY: Everyone knows.

RAY picks up the up-ended box.

RAY: I'm paying him back, alright.

TINY: Yeah.

As RAY picks up the box half its lid drops off.

RAY: Bugger.

And out fall several small bubble wrapped packages.

TINY: What are those.

RAY: I don't know.

RAY picks up a package

TINY: No, don't.

RAY unwraps a package.

RAY: Shotgun cartridges.

TINY: How did they get there.

69

RAY: I don't know.

RAY picks up large screwdriver and prises off remaining half of lid, takes out several more packages.

TINY: I don't like this.

RAY begins to prise open another box.

What's that.

RAY: Where.

TINY: On the stair.

Silence.

RAY: Nothing.

RAY opens box and takes out more packages.

TINY: We haven't seen anything we put them back and say nothing.

RAY throws TINY keys.

RAY: Go and lock up the van. Do it, now.

Exit TINY.

RAY prises open remaining boxes and finds more cartridges and pieces to make up a shotgun. Enter WATSON from kitchen.

Stanley.

WATSON: Where's the other one.

RAY: Look what we found. In your wine.

Silence.

WATSON: Where's the other one.

RAY: Shotgun cartridges. And a shotgun.

Silence.

What have you got in the garage, a tank.

WATSON: No, a Morris Minor one thousand – that's my wine, who said you could open my wine.

RAY: The lid fell off.

Enter TINY.

Shut the door.

TINY shuts door.

And keep it shut.

WATSON: This is my house.

RAY picks up crow bar from tool box.

RAY: Don't let him out of the room.

TINY: Where are you going.

RAY: To look in the garage.

Exit RAY.

TINY: Sit down if you like.

WATSON: I live here.

TINY: Suit yourself.

WATSON: This is my home.

Silence.

The council won't employ you again after this.

TINY: Let's open a bottle of wine.

WATSON: If you like.

WATSON makes for the door.

TINY: Where are you going.

WATSON: To get a corkscrew.

TINY: No, you're not.

WATSON: This is my house.

TINY: I'll get one.

TINY picks up a large screw driver.

That should do it. Sit down Stanley.

WATSON sits.

We'll have one of these.

Picks up bottle of wine.

WATSON: You'll never work again.

TINY: How much is this a bottle.

WATSON: I'll see you in hell.

TINY: How much.

WATSON: More than you can afford.

TINY: Don't get like that Stanley – it's not me, this is not my fault, I haven't done anything wrong.

TINY starts to open wine with screwdriver.

WATSON: I'll give you a reference, alright.

Silence.

You and your mate.

Silence.

He's not coming back. He won't come back.

TINY plunges cork.

He's gone.

TINY: You don't mind a mug do you.

WATSON: There's glasses in the kitchen.

TINY: We'll have mugs.

TINY pours wine and gives a mug to WATSON.

There you go.

WATSON: You'll pay for this.

TINY: I probably already am in an alternate universe, but
not in this universe pop, in this universe I can do what I
want. Cheers.

TINY drinks.

WATSON: This is an outrage.

TINY: You're not drinking. Drink your wine Stanley.

WATSON drinks.

WATSON: This is my home.

TINY: Call the police.

WATSON: Yes, I will.

TINY: Go on then.

Silence.

I'll do it for you if you like.

Silence.

WATSON: It's an outrage.

TINY: Have a drink.

They drink. Silence.

WATSON: My head hurts. This isn't any good for my head. I'm dying.

TINY: No, you're not.

Silence.

Stop looking at me like that. I said stop it. Stop looking at me. Stop it man.

WATSON: I'm not doing anything.

TINY: Stop looking at me – shut your eyes.

WATSON: Do I have to.

TINY: Yes.

WATSON: You'll hit me.

TINY: No I won't.

WATSON: I'm an old man.

TINY: Close your eyes.

WATSON: Do I have to.

TINY: Yes.

WATSON closes his eyes.

And don't open them until I say so.

Silence.

WATSON: Now what.

TINY: I don't know, alright – I don't know.

Silence.

WATSON: We could play 'I Spy'.

TINY: I said to keep them shut.

WATSON groans.

Silence. Enter RAY with a briefcase and a small portable concrete base with a length of copper piping set in it with a firing mechanism and a timing device.

I thought you'd gone, I didn't think you were coming back.

RAY sets concrete base on a wine box.

RAY: What has he got his eyes closed for.

TINY: Because I told him.

RAY: Open your eyes.

TINY: Open them Stanley.

WATSON opens his eyes.

WATSON: Go on, hit me.

TINY: What's that.

RAY: A bomb.

TINY: No, it's not.

RAY: It is, isn't it Stanley.

TINY: What did you bring it in here for.

RAY: To show Stanley.

WATSON: Hit me.

RAY: Why, what have you done.

TINY: Take it out.

RAY: You take it out.

TINY: I'm not taking it out you brought it in you take it out I'm not touching it, it's not safe it's a bomb.

WATSON: That's not a bomb.

TINY: It's a bomb.

RAY: What is it then.

WATSON: I don't know.

RAY: It was in your garage.

TINY: I knew we shouldn't have gone to France, I didn't want to go to France I hate the French.

RAY: What is it.

WATSON: I don't know.

TINY: How do you know it's not a bomb.

RAY: He made it.

WATSON: My head hurts.

RAY: What is it.

WATSON: I'm dying.

RAY: What have you got a machine gun in your garage for, what are all the empty fireworks for – what's the gunpowder for – the nails, the lead shot, the ball–bearings, the fuses, the timers – It's a bomb factory, your garage is a bomb factory.

WATSON: Go on then, hit me.

RAY lays the briefcase flat on the chair.

RAY: What's in the briefcase.

WATSON: I don't know.

RAY: Open it.

TINY: No, don't.

WATSON: You should call the police.

RAY: Open the briefcase.

WATSON: It might be a bomb.

RAY: Or money.

WATSON: I don't know.

RAY: Open it.

WATSON: You're sure.

RAY: Yes.

TINY: No.

WATSON: How do you know it's not a bomb.

RAY: You won't open it if it is.

WATSON: I've never seen this briefcase before in my life.

RAY: Open it.

TINY: Oh fuck.

WATSON stands over briefcase.

Silence.

It's a bomb.

RAY: Open it.

Silence.

WATSON snaps up the fasteners.

TINY: Yargh.

RAY: Now open it slowly, very slowly and keep your hands on the lid where I can see them at all times.

WATSON opens lid very slowly.

Now step away.

RAY goes to briefcase and looks in it. It's full of black and white photographs of varying sizes.

Where is it Stanley.

TINY: I have to go.

RAY: No, you don't.

TINY: Yes, I do. I do, I've got an appointment. I can't just not go, they know me.

RAY: So ring them up and cancel it.

TINY: I have to go.

RAY: Ring them up Tiny, do it now.

TINY goes to phone and dials. RAY picks up a clutch of photographs from briefcase, shuffles through them and describes them one by one.

Bank – Bank – Supermarket – Bank – Old lady with shopping – Bank – Telephone box – Supermarket – Supermarket...

TINY: Yeah, I want to cancel an appointment.

RAY looks at back of a photograph.

Eight o'clock.

RAY: (*Reads back of photo.*) '24–0–1. Telephone box Temple Fortune BB, explosive, detonated one fifty-eight, no injuries.'

Looks at back of another photograph.

TINY: Yeah, that's right I'm not coming.

RAY: (*Reads.*) '13–11, Flowerbed SS Dog Kennel Hill, Shotgun detonated four thirty-two, shrapnel injury one shopper.'

TINY: No I'm bloody not and you can't make me neither

TINY puts down phone.

WATSON: I'm not ashamed, I've got nothing to be ashamed of.

TINY: I'm not paying a cancellation fee how can they make me pay if I don't go back.

WATSON: I've done nothing wrong.

TINY: I want a woman in my bed not in my life, she's a prostitute, that's the point.

WATSON: My conscience is clear.

Silence.

RAY: So, where's all the money.

WATSON: What money.

TINY: Yeah, he would say that.

RAY: Where do you keep the money Stanley.

WATSON: There is no money.

TINY: No, no – what about all those demands for huge amounts of money.

WATSON: They haven't paid.

RAY: How can you afford this.

WATSON: I can't.

TINY: There'll be a reward for him.

WATSON: I'm in the middle of negotiations.

TINY: Like yeah, they've got your telephone number.

WATSON: Covert negotiations through coded messages in the newspaper.

RAY: I'll ring the police.

WATSON: They're arranging for me to have access to a million pounds.

RAY: What do you mean access.

WATSON: The method of payment.

TINY: You get them to put it in a brown paper bag and leave it in a bin somewhere, this is rubbish.

TINY picks up phone.

WATSON: Benefit cheats expose bomber, that'll make good copy.

TINY puts phone down.

RAY: We haven't killed anyone.

WATSON: Neither have I.

TINY: If that old lady dies you will have. They'll lock you up and throw away the key, grandad.

WATSON: They'll do you for fraud.

RAY: Did you love your mother unnaturally Stanley. I did, my love for my mother was definitely unnatural. It was Oedipal, I wanted to fuck her. When she married my stepfather I wanted to kill him and fuck her. I've read the Guardian, I've had therapy.

TINY: He had a posh girlfriend.

RAY: We're not imbeciles.

TINY: He went to a mad group for five years and then they asked him to leave.

RAY: Where's the money Stanley.

WATSON: There is no money.

RAY: Stanley.

WATSON: If there was money I'd give you money.

RAY: I like you, Stanley. This is not personal, it's got nothing to do with personalities.

WATSON: No.

RAY: So, where's the money.

WATSON: I'm thirsty.

RAY: After you've told me where the money is.

WATSON: Fetch me a glass of water.

RAY: Where is the money Stanley.

TINY: Tell him where the money is Stanley.

WATSON: There isn't any.

RAY: Right.

RAY rolls back his sleeves.

TINY: No.

RAY: You see Stanley, I've had therapy and Tiny hasn't.

WATSON: Upstairs.

RAY: Yes.

WATSON: Upstairs, by my bed – there's a newspaper.

RAY: Stop taking the piss.

WATSON: I'm not.

RAY: You are.

TINY: He's not.

RAY: He doesn't leave the room, you don't leave the room, you watch him.

Exit RAY.

TINY: It's his ex-wife. She's got a new boyfriend. You don't look like a terrorist Stanley.

WATSON: I'm not.

TINY: You plant bombs.

Silence.

WATSON: It is not and never has been my intention to injure or harm anyone, in part the object of the whole operation has been to provide me with mental stimulation and an outlet for my expertise in marketing sales and public relations. And I don't like banks. I'm thirsty.

TINY: Have some wine.

WATSON: I need water.

TINY: After.

WATSON: After what.

TINY: When he's come back.

Silence.

WATSON: Just a glass of water. My teeth hurt and I've got stomach-ache.

TINY: You'll have to wait.

WATSON: I can't.

TINY: You have to.

Silence.

WATSON: After my wife died, I got very low, very depressed. I swam out to sea to drown in January and was dragged back in by the current, sideways back up a river into a jetty and pulled myself out. I was in my swimming trunks, in the middle of January.

TINY: Cold. Well it would be. It was wasn't it.

WATSON: Yes. I was fifty-five years old and I thought if ever I'm going to do something I'd better do it now. I was going to build a boat.

TINY: Like Noah. What happened.

WATSON: Fetch me a glass of water.

TINY: No.

WATSON: Please.

TINY: No.

Sound of floorboards coming up.

And what about God.

WATSON: What about him.

TINY: I don't know. When did you stop going to church.

WATSON: The Bible was my church. I don't like the way
that the Anglicans let homosexuals and women preach,
and who are Catholic priests that they can forgive me –
if I need forgiveness I go straight to God not a box with
a man in it.

TINY: What do you believe in now.

WATSON: Bits of dust and atoms.

TINY: Just as well.

WATSON: I'm tired, I've got stomach-ache, my teeth hurt
and I'm thirsty.

Sound of breaking furniture.

TINY: I used to have a problem with the idea of God – and
then I got to thinking and I realised that we're all part
of the same universal mind, that we're all part of the
same energy – like dogs sensing things in the dark and
ESP, it's all the same thing – we are God, we're all God.

WATSON gives TINY a card.

WATSON: My card.

TINY reads it.

TINY: (*Reading card.*) 'Welcome to the Association and the Associate Experience, Yours sincerely, The Associate.' I like the logo.

WATSON: All of my clients get one.

TINY: Double O seven.

WATSON: It's a calling card, it's packaging, it's marketing, it's good PR, a brand name, a label, a mark of quality, a guarantee of satisfaction, an absolute unshakeable and certain belief in the product, put the fear of God into them with a smile on your face.

TINY gives it back.

Keep it.

TINY: Thanks.

WATSON clutches stomach and groans.

What's the matter.

WATSON groans.

Stop it – stop doing that.

WATSON: I need a glass of water.

TINY: No.

WATSON: I won't move, I can't move.

TINY: Stop asking will you, I've said haven't I, haven't I, I've said – I'll hit you if you don't stop – is that what you want, you want me to hit you – do you – well do you.

WATSON: No.

Silence.

Sound of banging and breaking furniture offstage. TINY takes out chewing gum.

TINY: Have a bit of gum. Go on, it's Juicy Fruit.

WATSON takes a bit.

WATSON: Thank you.

TINY takes a bit and puts it in his mouth.

TINY: Do you like Juicy Fruit.

WATSON: No.

Loud crash of breaking glass.

TINY: The reason why I eat chewing gum is when I have a cigarette to take away the smell afterwards – when I'm on a date you know out of consideration.

WATSON groans.

I don't want to hit you but I will if I have to.

Silence.

I eat two sometimes.

Banging from upstairs.

He's having trouble finding your paper. Are you a socialist.

WATSON: I've got no time for politics or politicians, whatever they do it doesn't affect me, my life continues the same whoever they are. What do you vote for.

TINY: Nothing, I don't.

WATSON: The Catholic Church is buying a big telescope so that it can look deep into space back to the beginning of the universe the big bang the hand of God.

TINY: I'll be interested to know what they find out.

Enter RAY with newspaper.

What did you find.

RAY: Nothing.

RAY thrusts paper at WATSON.

Your newspaper.

WATSON takes paper.

TINY: Calm, calm.

RAY: Go on then.

TINY: Calm.

RAY: I am calm, I'm calm, alright.

TINY: Alright.

RAY: Well.

WATSON gives paper to RAY.

WATSON: The ad at the top.

RAY: (*Reads.*) 'A. Work started on plan for London delivery of one million news letters. Earliest target date mid-April. Hope this fits with your schedule. B.' Who's B.

WATSON: The police.

RAY: There isn't any money.

WATSON: No.

RAY pours himself wine.

I'm dying.

RAY: You look fit enough to me.

WATSON: Every time I go out that door it might be my last, I might never come back.

TINY: Yeah, you might get caught.

WATSON: Or drop dead.

TINY: You're not dying.

WATSON: I'm dying.

RAY: What are you dying of.

WATSON: A rare brain disorder.

RAY: What's this brain disorder called.

WATSON: I don't know, they won't tell me. They don't want me to know. I had a stroke, they said it was a matter of months.

RAY: When was this.

WATSON: Two years ago.

RAY: You're not dying.

WATSON: That's easy for you to say. Go on, torture me.

TINY: We're not going to torture you, why would we torture you, Dad.

WATSON: You've got no principles.

TINY: He had one of those on his foot, they had to remove it with surgery.

WATSON: How much do you want.

RAY: We might not be for sale.

TINY: Yeah, we might not have got any principles but we're not cheap.

WATSON: How much.

RAY: One million pounds.

WATSON: Half.

RAY: All of it, you give us all the money Stanley and we'll say nothing.

Silence.

TINY: Those eyes man, they've been haunting me all day – those eyes would haunt anyone.

Silence.

WATSON: I accept.

RAY: Right.

TINY: Right.

RAY: A million pounds.

WATSON: Yes.

TINY: Yeah.

Silence.

What does it look like.

RAY: I don't know.

TINY: Yeah.

Silence.

I need a drink.

RAY: Have some wine.

TINY: No, a proper drink.

RAY: Yeah.

RAY picks up shotgun cartridges.

TINY: What are you doing.

RAY: Putting them safe.

TINY: Right.

RAY: We'll put these boxes back in the van.

RAY and TINY put everything back in wine boxes.

It's your round.

TINY: I haven't got any money.

RAY: Only half a million pounds.

TINY: Yeah.

RAY: Yeah.

They laugh.

Here, Stan –

TINY: Yeah Stan, Stan the man.

RAY: Why go to France to buy a shotgun and cartridges.

WATSON: It's dangerous to buy suspicious components close to home.

TINY: I can buy a Porsche, or a Lambourghini Diablo – both – and a Ferrari, and a Lotus Elan.

WATSON: You don't talk about this outside the house.

TINY: One million pounds.

WATSON: This is the only place we talk about it.

RAY: Whatever you say Stan.

TINY: You are the man Stan, Stan the man, I love you Stan.

WATSON: And after, when you've got the money how do I know you won't say anything.

RAY: You don't, you have to trust us Stanley.

TINY: Yeah.

RAY: Yeah.

WATSON: Yes

TINY: I'll open the van.

Exit TINY with box.

RAY: What is the method of payment.

WATSON: On a given day a leading supermarket will issue thousands of free plastic discount cards with a variety of national consumer magazines. Any one of these cards when used with a secret pin number will allow me to make withdrawals from cash machines all over Britain; up to one million pounds.

RAY: And how do we know you won't just walk off with it.

WATSON: You don't, you have to trust me.

RAY: I'm going to write all this down Stanley and put it in an envelope, to be opened in the event of any accident I might meet with.

RAY picks up box.

You can fill in all the cracks for us over night, so we can start papering as soon as we get in tomorrow. See you about lunchtime.

Exit RAY with a box.

Silence.

Sound of front door closing.

WATSON looks out window. Draws curtains. Takes crow bar and lifts up a section of floorboards and takes out large bundles of twenty pound notes.

Scene 2

Afternoon. Room nearly lined with lining paper. Two more strips and it will be done. TINY at wallpaper table cutting and pasting lining paper and folding it ready for hanging, talks as he works. RAY up step-ladder waiting for lining paper to hang. During scene day turns to dusk fading to night.

RAY: He swaggers.

TINY: He's a big head.

RAY: And when he gets angry, when he doesn't get what he wants he turns into an old woman.

TINY: At least he didn't break your legs.

RAY: He knows he'll get his money.

TINY: His wife's alright. I like his wife.

RAY: I don't know how she puts up with it.

TINY: What did you tell him.

RAY: Nothing, that the council had offered us a big contract beginning the end of April with a load of cash up front.

TINY: I could shag his wife.

RAY: Yeah.

TINY: Yeah.

RAY: Yeah.

TINY: Yeah, yeah I will, I'll shag his wife, shag his wife and wipe the smile off his face.

RAY: And then I'll shag her.

TINY: After.

RAY: After – and we'll make him watch.

TINY: Yeah.

RAY: Yeah, I'll teach him how to shag his wife.

TINY: And she'll beg for more.

RAY: And he'll cry.

TINY: Wipe the smile off his face.

TINY gives folded lining paper to RAY.

RAY: Ta.

RAY hangs paper, talks as he works. TINY opens the office and takes out a can of lager.

TINY: That's it, the stationery cupboard's empty.

TINY opens lager.

RAY: We'll knock off after this wall.

TINY: We only got here an hour ago.

RAY: I'm celebrating, it's my daughter's birthday. We could get Stanley to wipe the smile off his face permanently.

TINY: Oh no, wo-wo-wo, I'm not blowing anyone up.

RAY: One Eyed Baz, the mother of my child, traffic wardens, the landlord at the Raven, that smug bastard down the dole –

TINY: Which one.

RAY: With the ring through his nose.

TINY: Oh, yeah.

RAY: The skinny girl from the chip shop.

TINY: That blonde wanker off the telly, we could strap him to a bomb and say, 'Now who wants to be a millionaire, cunt.'

RAY: Yeah.

TINY: Yeah.

They laugh.

Enter WATSON with laundry basket.

WATSON: I don't see what there's to laugh at.

RAY: How's my money coming on.

WATSON puts basket to one side, takes out a bottle of red wine and puts it on wallpapering table.

WATSON: Go on then, take it.

RAY: What for.

WATSON: It's vintage Beaujolais.

RAY: What for.

WATSON: He said you were going to a party.

TINY: We are.

RAY: Yeah, straight after work.

WATSON: It's a present.

RAY: You're not coming.

WATSON: I don't want to.

RAY: It's my daughter's birthday, it's a children's party.

WATSON: Don't have it then.

RAY: No, we'll have it. And the rest.

WATSON: I'll be glad to see the back of you.

RAY: Misery guts.

WATSON: Drop dead.

WATSON sits at table and picks at teeth with a tooth pick.

TINY: He's happy.

RAY: Yeah, what are you happy about, dad.

TINY: He is, he's grinning.

WATSON: Drop dead the pair of you.

TINY/RAY: (*Together.*) Ooooh.

TINY: You drop dead grandad.

RAY: Yeah, and wipe that grin off your face, it's unnatural.

WATSON: My teeth hurt.

TINY: He's been listening to those old records of his again.

RAY: And stop dribbling.

TINY: He can't help it man, it's his brain.

RAY: Brain what brain it's all mush, he's demolished it – he can't even pick up a cup of tea without shaking – you've been on the sauce too long grandad – you know what you are don't you, you're a mirage, you're not here and we don't exist.

WATSON: At least I'm not fat.

RAY: I could have you no trouble.

WATSON: Yeah.

RAY: Yeah.

WATSON: Not if I saw you coming first you wouldn't.

TINY: Did you have long hair in the sixties, dad.

WATSON: No.

RAY: He's always had no hair

WATSON: I'll have you, see if I don't.

RAY: I thought you were dying.

WATSON: It's a miracle I've survived this long.

RAY: You can do some pasting, we might go down the pub.

WATSON: You're never out that pub.

RAY: I like your pub Stanley, it's a pound a pint at lunch time and they've got strippers.

WATSON: Are they live.

TINY: No, they're dead – what sort of women are you used to.

WATSON: You should put that wine somewhere safe, somewhere you won't forget – I'll put it in a bag for you.

RAY: Not bloody likely.

RAY opens office and puts wine in. Shuts office.

That's safe.

WATSON: I'll be glad to see the back of you.

RAY: The sooner you get us our money the sooner we're gone. How much longer do we have to wait.

WATSON: Two more weeks.

RAY: It's always two more weeks with you, I don't trust you, I don't see what the problem is.

WATSON: It's complicated, arrangements have to be made.

RAY: What arrangements, all they have to do is print a load of plastic saver cards.

WATSON: My teeth hurt.

TINY: You're not dying.

WATSON: Each day could be my last.

TINY: Live for the moment, Stan.

WATSON: I've hardly lived my life and now it's nearly the end.

TINY: Stan. (*Laughs.*)

RAY: How do you live for the moment.

TINY: Have loads of sex.

RAY: Do you have loads of sex, Stanley.

TINY: Well, do you.

WATSON: No.

RAY: No.

WATSON: I get these thoughts.

RAY: You should get a bike instead, dad.

TINY: Yeah, you'd be less dangerous.

RAY: No, more.

TINY: Yeah.

> *RAY and TINY laugh.*

WATSON: All the things I thought I was going to be.

RAY: Nothing like a good bike ride for clearing away the cobwebs.

TINY: Yeah, or loads of pornography.

> *WATSON makes to go.*

RAY: The old lady you put in a coma, they turned off her life support machine this morning.

> *Silence.*

WATSON: I'll put the washing on.

RAY: You can do all my washing from now on.

TINY: And mine. Do you iron. Well. Do you, do you do ironing.

WATSON: Yes.

TINY: Right. He does ironing. I'll bring a load of shirts in then.

RAY: You can help finish this wall.

WATSON: I've got the washing to do.

RAY: It's your house, it's your mess we're covering up.

TINY: Yeah, Stan, this is your home you live here.

WATSON: I have to do my washing.

RAY: We haven't got any money, how much money have you got on you.

WATSON: I don't know.

RAY: Well look in your pockets.

TINY: He said look in your pockets.

RAY: Look in his pockets.

WATSON: No, no – it's alright, I can manage.

RAY: Don't get lippy.

WATSON: No, I'm not.

WATSON looks in pockets.

A twenty pound note.

RAY: That's lucky.

TINY: Yeah, dead lucky.

RAY: That's how much we need.

TINY takes money.

TINY: Do you want anything from the shop Stanley.

WATSON: No, no thanks.

Exit TINY.

How old's your daughter.

RAY: Three.

WATSON: Three's a nice age.

RAY: Yeah she's fantastic, I really love her. I need that money Stanley, and I need it now.

WATSON: For your ex-wife.

RAY: No, and we never got married.

WATSON: Why not.

RAY: I never fancied it – she thinks that the world owes her a living, that she's been done some injury suffered some pain – so you can't talk to her...she won't talk she doesn't talk she screams –

WATSON: You still love her.

RAY: I never loved her.

WATSON: You must have loved her once.

RAY: How much would it cost to give her a fright.

WATSON: You want me to send something in the post to her.

RAY: Nothing serious, just enough to shock her.

WATSON: Why, what's she done.

RAY: Nothing she hasn't done anything, forget it.

RAY kicks chair over.

Just get the money.

Exit RAY.

WATSON picks up the office, opens it, and removes the wine. As he does, he sees a sealed envelope in the office, picks it up and reads the address.

WATSON: (*Aloud.*) 'To whom it may concern in the event of my untimely death. Raymond Povey.'

WATSON puts envelope back in the office. He takes out a bundle of washing from laundry basket and unwraps a bomb with detonator, fits bomb securely into the office with detonator primed to go off when the lid is opened, closes the office and hides wine in laundry basket.

Enter TINY with cans of lager.

WATSON quickly gets behind wallpapering table and measures out paper.

Dusk outside fading to night.

TINY sits at table.

Sound of toilet flushing offstage.

TINY opens can of lager.

TINY: Three steps to heaven – double gin, double whiskey, double vodka, all at seventy-five pence a shot.

Enter RAY with newspaper.

RAY: Where have you been.

TINY: I stopped off for a drink.

RAY sits and reads paper.

WATSON measures, cuts and pastes lining paper ready for hanging as they talk.

She's infatuated with me, she adores me, it's embarassing, I can't get rid of her. I can't just tell her to get lost, she's done nothing wrong. She says she'll do anything for me, whatever I want – I'm not into all that rubbish, I'm into equality, I want an equal relationship.

RAY: You want a woman with balls.

TINY: Yeah. Of course I also realise that women come with more sophisticated needs than men.

RAY: Oh, yeah.

TINY: Yeah.

RAY: And what are these sophisticated needs.

TINY: Well, they're – it's not just all physical with them – I don't know, I'm not an expert on women.

RAY: No. You use prostitutes.

TINY: I've offered to get you one, but you won't.

WATSON: No he wouldn't, that would be like admitting to his mates that he's useless at pulling the girls.

RAY: I don't need to pull anyone.

TINY: I'm not useless.

WATSON: I never said you were.

RAY: Who asked you to say anything. I know what your game is.

TINY: I've been thinking about why you won't go with a prostitute, it's because your mother was a woman.

RAY: And yours wasn't.

TINY: No, no – it's not as stupid as it sounds.

RAY: Yes it is.

TINY: Anyway, I told her, I said I won't be around for much longer. I said I had a rich uncle who was dying in Australia, who had a sheep farm and he was leaving it all to me by the end of April.

WATSON: What else did you tell her.

TINY: Nothing.

RAY: You just concentrate on getting us our money.

TINY: I get this urge, a physical need.

RAY: Hurry them up, Stanley

WATSON: I'm trying.

RAY: Negotiate faster.

TINY: It takes over – deciding where to go, getting out the money, where from, which cash machine, the cash in my pocket, how am I going to get there, what bus, what train, what time, what place, handing over the money – and I'm thinking about it all day, and no one else knows, they don't know I'm going to see a prostitute.

WATSON: What about the sex.

TINY: Yeah, it's alright. You must feel like that about your job – all the planning and waiting and expectation.

WATSON: I always wear the same gloves and jacket when carrying a bomb to its intended site.

TINY: What for.

WATSON: Luck.

RAY: Just tell them you want the money now, or else.

TINY: Where are my keys, I've lost my keys.

RAY: No you haven't.

TINY: I have, I've lost my keys.

RAY: When did you last have them.

TINY: I don't remember, I can't find my keys I've lost my keys. Look in the office.

RAY: You always do this.

TINY: Help me look for my keys.

RAY: You haven't lost them.

TINY: Just look will you.

RAY: Alright.

TINY rifles through his pockets.

RAY picks up the office.

WATSON: I'll look in the hall.

TINY: They're not in the hall.

RAY: Yeah, you stay where you are.

RAY unfastens clasps to office and is about to raise the lid.

TINY: Got them.

TINY pulls keys out of jacket pocket.

RAY: Plank.

WATSON: Yes.

RAY: Have you written to the council yet.

WATSON: No.

RAY: You can do that tonight then.

WATSON: Have you written your letter yet.

RAY: Yes, yes Stanley I have.

WATSON: Where have you put it.

RAY: Somewhere safe.

RAY refastens clasps on the office.

TINY: I'm always doing that, I'm always losing my keys, what does it mean.

WATSON: Why does it have to mean anything.

TINY: No, no, it definitely means something.

WATSON begins folding paper.

RAY: (*Reads headline from newspaper.*) 'Man arrested after woman found in suitcase at Heathrow airport.' Friend of yours, Stan.

WATSON: I think not.

RAY: You don't like women, he doesn't like women does he.

TINY: No.

RAY: See, you don't like women.

WATSON: I was married.

RAY: And she left you.

TINY: She hung herself.

RAY: Yeah, it was the only way out. You killed your wife.

TINY: He killed his wife.

RAY: You haven't got any family.

WATSON has finished folding paper.

RAY up stepladder. WATSON gives RAY lining paper.

TINY: I've only got my dad.

RAY: Be nice to us Stanley, be very nice.

RAY hangs lining paper and talks as he works.

TINY: He hit us with anything he could lay his hands on – slippers, broom handles, fists, but not a belt, never a belt, he didn't wear a belt.

RAY: Oh no, he's getting sentimental about his dad.

WATSON: My father never laid a finger on me.

RAY: And look what happened.

WATSON: He was a gentle man, he worked on the trams.

RAY: You said he was a cook.

WATSON: Yes, he was – after. He was a quiet man, he didn't complain, I never heard him complain; he fell drunk off Blackfriars Bridge one morning and drowned.

RAY: My dad hit me and it didn't do me any harm, I deserved a good hiding.

TINY: I says to him, I said, 'If you hate children so much, how come you had me.' I was eight years old and he broke my arm.

RAY: Who would we tell Stanley if anything happened to you.

WATSON: You could tell my son.

RAY: You said your wife couldn't have children.

WATSON: She couldn't.

RAY: You cheated on your wife.

WATSON: No.

RAY: You knocked up some poor girl and then left her.

TINY: I woke up one morning and he was gone.

RAY: And he says he hasn't lived.

WATSON: He was conceived in a caravan in Primrose Valley, halfway between Bridlington and Scarborough. His mother sends photographs, I used to send money.

RAY: Where is he now.

WATSON: He works in a shoe factory just outside Kettering.

RAY: I don't trust you.

TINY: He fucked off. He fucked off and left us.

RAY: You're not dying.

WATSON: I'll see you both in hell.

TINY: And then he came back. What are you grinning at.

WATSON: Nothing.

TINY: Wipe that grin off your face.

WATSON: I'm not grinning.

TINY: Stop grinning.

WATSON: I'm not.

TINY: I said stop it. You think this is funny. Do you, well do you – do you think this is funny.

WATSON: No.

TINY: No it's not bloody funny, you're not funny, what are you.

WATSON: I don't know.

TINY: Not funny, stop grinning.

WATSON: My teeth hurt.

RAY: You should see a dentist.

TINY: Maybe I should take a look.

Picks up a pair of pliers.

I've always fancied myself as a dentist.

RAY: Yeah, a mental hygenist.

WATSON: It's hysterical toothache.

RAY: Why aren't you laughing then.

TINY: He's not laughing.

TINY places chair in middle of room.

Sit down Stanley.

WATSON: I'm better standing up

TINY: Sit down.

WATSON: No, it's alright, I'm alright.

RAY: What's the matter Stanley.

WATSON: Nothing.

TINY: Sit down.

RAY: Sit.

WATSON sits.

TINY: Now let's have a look at your teeth. Open your mouth.

WATSON sits still.

Open it, Stanley.

WATSON remains still.

Open your mouth.

WATSON keeps still.

How can we help you if you won't open your mouth.

TINY holds WATSON's head in armlock and brings pliers up to WATSON's mouth.

Open it.

WATSON struggles.

Keep still will you.

They fall to floor. TINY sits astride watson, trapping him face up.

Stop wriggling – he's got ants in his pants, you've got ants in your pants Stanley and they're having a dance – now, show me your teeth.

Telephone rings. RAY answers it.

RAY: Hello…no…no, we don't…yeah…that's alright.

Puts down telephone.

TINY: Who was it.

RAY: I don't know.

TINY: What did they want.

RAY: A pizza.

TINY gets up.

TINY: The look on your face, man. The look on his face. He thought I was going to pull out all your teeth with a pair of pliers Stanley.

RAY: Yeah.

TINY: Yeah.

They laugh.

I'm mad me, I just do mad things.

RAY: Yeah, he takes after his dad.

TINY: No, I don't. Yeah. (*Laughs.*) It was only a bit of fun Stan, I'd have to be scum to do something like that.

RAY: Yeah, total scum.

TINY: I'll buy you a drink.

WATSON: I'm not thirsty.

RAY: We want our money now Stanley.

TINY: Yeah, now.

WATSON: I'm trying.

RAY: Try harder.

WATSON: There are still details to be finalised.

RAY: I'm going to my daughter's birthday party now, but I'll be back after, I'm moving in until we get the money, I don't trust you.

WATSON: I don't trust you.

RAY and TINY go to exit.

Don't forget your office.

WATSON gives RAY the office.

RAY: I'm watching you.

TINY: Here, put these in it.

Picks up cans of lager.

WATSON: You're going to be late.

RAY: You're up to something, he's up to something, I'm going to watch over you night and day.

WATSON: Will your wife be at the party.

RAY: You just get us our money Stanley and we won't pull out all your teeth with a pair of pliers.

TINY: Yeah. Put these in the office.

RAY: Carry them yourself, lazy bugger.

RAY exits followed by TINY.

TINY: Can I drive.

RAY: No.

TINY: Why not.

RAY: I'll hit you.

They exit.

TINY: (*Off.*) What for – you hit me.

RAY: (*Off.*) I said.

Sound of front door closing after them.

Silence.

WATSON looks out the window. Night. Takes a travelling bag and overcoat out from under the table, takes mirror out of bag sits to table and puts on false beard and moustache and glasses, puts on overcoat and hat, takes a copy of 'Loot' from one of the pockets, spreads it on the pasting table and rips out a plastic discount card, puts on gloves, picks up bag and makes to leave. Stops and goes over to paper lined wall, opens tin of red primer and paints a big red circle on the wall, on top of the circle he paints a large red capital A forming the symbol for anarchy. In smaller block capitals running across from the 'A' he paints the letters 's-s-o-c-i-a-t-e'.

Exit WATSON with bag.

The End.